T·H·E
PERFECTLY ORDERLY
H·O·U·S·E

Ellen Kindt McKenzie

Illustrated by
Megan Lloyd

Henry Holt and Company / New York

To Elizabeth Popp and Pat Wood
—E.K.M.

To Jane, Steve, and Nicholas
—M.L.

Henry Holt and Company, Inc.
Publishers since 1866
115 West 18th Street
New York, New York 10011
Henry Holt is a registered
trademark of Henry Holt and Company, Inc.
Text copyright © 1994 by Ellen Kindt McKenzie
Illustrations copyright © 1994 by Megan Lloyd
All rights reserved.
Published in Canada by Fitzhenry & Whiteside Ltd.,
195 Allstate Parkway, Markham, Ontario L3R 4T8.

Library of Congress Cataloging-in-Publication Data
McKenzie, Ellen Kindt.
A perfectly orderly house / Ellen Kindt McKenzie ;
illustrated by Megan Lloyd.
Summary: An old woman builds a house with twenty-six rooms
and keeps all her possessions in alphabetical order, but
she still can't find anything.
[1. Alphabet—Fiction.   2. Orderliness—Fiction.
3. Humorous stories.]   I. Lloyd, Megan, ill.   II. Title.
PZ7.M478676Pe   1994   [E]—dc20   93-42264

ISBN 0-8050-1946-4

First Edition—1994
Printed in the United States of America
on acid-free paper. ∞
1   3   5   7   9   10   8   6   4   2

The artist used color inks on vellum
to create the illustrations for this book.

There was an Old Woman who lived in a small bit of a house. The house would have been just right, for she was a small bit of a woman, except she could throw nothing away.

"For," she said, "what you throw away today, you'll surely need tomorrow."

And she was right. Except at last the house was so crowded the Old Woman couldn't find a thing she needed.

One day she cried, "It takes me so long hunting for what I've saved, I never get anything done. I never have time for a party. I need a more orderly house."

She thought a bit. Then she said, "There is nothing more orderly than the alphabet. Everything I have begins with one letter or another. I'll just put it all in the order of the ABC's."

So she arranged everything in her closet and cupboard and icebox. Aprons, Blouses, Coats. Bowls, Cups, Dinner plates. Eggs, Fudge, Garlic.

And so she did with everything else in the house.

But though it was orderly, she couldn't always get at
what she wanted. One day she cried, "I need my quilt, but
it's under the piano. This won't do! I need a big house with
all the rooms in the order of the alphabet. Everything that
starts with *A* will go into the *A* room. Everything that
starts with *B* will go into the *B* room. *That* will be orderly."

She called her brother Sam, who was a carpenter, and
asked him to build her a perfectly orderly house.

"First room first, Sam," she told him. "Start here beside
the fence and build the Attic."

Sam scratched his head. But once the Old Woman wanted something, no arguing would stop her. Sam built the Attic to keep her quiet.

"I can hardly wait for the house to be finished," said the Old Woman as she brought the Aprons to the Attic. "When it is, I shall have a big party. Dig a hole for the Basement, Sam."

While the Old Woman was packing a Box of Bowls for the Basement, she called to Sam, "I just remembered, you must put the Bathroom in the Basement! Then make a large Closet for lots of things. Cat, Canary, and everything else that starts with *C*."

Sam built a very large Closet, and after that, the Dining room.

"Why are you putting your Dresses in the Dining room?" Sam asked. "Isn't the Closet big enough?"

"Dresses start with *D*," said the Old Woman, "and so does Doorbell. Put the Doorbell in the Dining room, and finish the Entryway."

"What will you put in the Entryway?" Sam asked.

"Eggs," she said. "For the cake for the party."

"Hmmm," Sam said. He finished the Entryway, and went on to build the Family room and the Garage.

"Shall I put your car in the Garage?" he asked.

"No, Car starts with *C*," the Old Woman said.

"But the Closet isn't big enough," he argued. "And you can't get an Automobile into the Attic."

"I'll find a place for it," she said.

Sam shrugged. He built the Hallway and then went to find Ice for the Igloo.

By now the house went along the fence to the bottom of
the hill.

"I have to have a Junk room," said the Old Woman,
"because I have a lot of things that are Just Junk. All I have
to do is decide which things they are."

"I'm glad I don't have to decide," said Sam.

Sam got on with the Junk room, the Kitchen, and the
Laundry room, all going up the hill. The Music room went
across the top of the hill. As fast as Sam could build, the
Old Woman put things away. She scolded the moving men.
"You know the piano doesn't belong in the Music room!"

Next Sam built the Nautical knickknack room for their great-uncle's Nautical knickknacks, and then the Observatory and the Parlor.

"You don't have a Bedroom," he told the Old Woman, while the moving men put the piano where it belonged.

The Old Woman thought hard. Then she told Sam, "I shall have a Quiet room with a Quilt on a Queen-size bed."

So Sam built the Quiet room, and then he built the Rumpus room and the Study.

When the men brought the Rocking chair to the Rumpus room, Sam put his foot down. "That's my Restful chair. I don't want it in the Rumpus room."

"It starts with *R,*" said the Old Woman.

"I'll not nail another board to this house if they don't take it back," Sam said.

"You're getting tired and crotchety," said the Old Woman. "We'll bring the Couch from the Closet so you can take a nap on the Sofa in the Study." And I'll move the rocking chair later, she thought.

"*Me* crotchety! Humph!" said Sam.

After his nap, he built the Tennis court.

Now the house ran along the fence and up the hill and across the top and down the hill to the river.

"What's next?" Sam asked.

"The Understudy," she told him. "Because the Study needs propping up. After that, build the Vestibule."

"And what will you keep in the Vestibule?" Sam asked.

"A Variety of Vehicles," she told him, "including the one I drive to town."

The Old Woman thought about what she would have for
her party while she waited for Sam to build the Waiting
room. Then she waited in the Waiting room to see that Sam
made the X-ray room walls out of lead.

"Do you have an X-ray machine?" Sam asked.

"Not yet, but I may get one some day. I couldn't throw it
away just because I didn't have room for it. Now I need a
Yard for the Yardarm from our great-uncle's Yacht."

"Sloop," said Sam.

"Yardarm starts with a *Y*. It belongs on a Yacht."

Sam yawned and put up the Yardarm behind the X-ray
room. He was glad the Yard wasn't much work.

Finally Sam put a fence around the meadow. "It'll make a
fine Zoo," he said, "in case you ever need one."

"And now I can have my party!" cried the Old Woman.

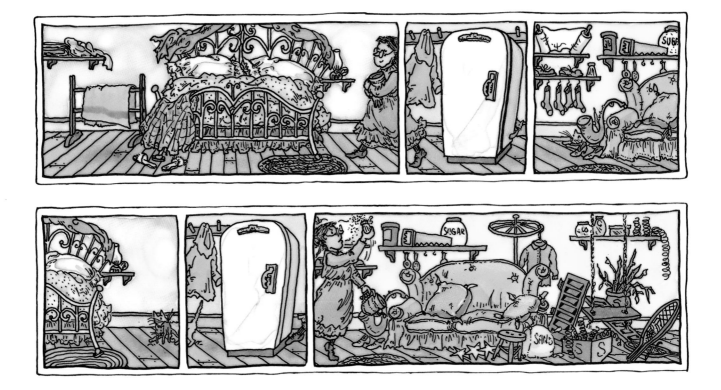

Off she went to the Kitchen to make the cake.

She went to the Study for the Sifter. She went back again for the Salt. Then she looked for the Milk.

"Oh dear," she cried. "The Milk is not in the Music room!" After a minute she remembered. "I put it in the Refrigerator in the Rumpus room so it wouldn't get sour. Isn't it fine to know where everything is!"

Back she went to the Study for the Sugar. Then she was off to find the Butter and the Baking powder. "It saved me steps remembering they were both in the Basement," she told herself.

At last the batter was in the pan. She took it to the Observatory to put in the Oven. She sat on the Ottoman to rest.

Finally all was ready. The Old Woman sat on the Ice chest in the Igloo, writing Invitations to everyone in town. She put them in the Mailbox outside the Music room at the top of the hill.

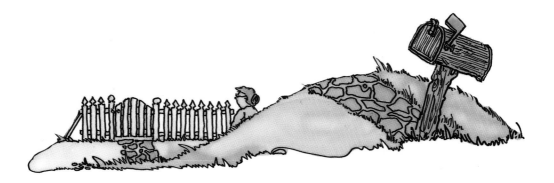

The next day everyone came to her party. Sam came too.

"This way!" the Old Woman called from the Attic. "The party will start after I show you the house."

It took almost forever to see all of the rooms. Everyone was hungry by the time they arrived at the Zoo.

"Are there cookies?" the children asked.

"Cookies and Cakes and Cold cuts are in the Closet," the Old Woman told them. "Children belong in the Closet too."

"Where is the ice cream?" they cried.

"In the Igloo," she told them.

Everyone looked everywhere for party things. They found Plates and Knives and Forks and Spoons and Napkins. By then they were hungrier than ever, so they looked for things to eat.

Appetizers were in the Attic, Hamburgers and Hot dogs in the Hallway. They hunted for Mustard and Ketchup. They found Turkey and Bread and Lettuce and Pickles in unexpected places.

The Old Woman told them that the Ladies should eat in the Laundry room. The Men took their plates to the Music room. Some Men were Gentlemen. They ate in the Garage. A Woman took her Potato salad from the Parlor to the Waiting room. Other Women were there. They all talked about the party.

"It's like a treasure hunt!" they said.

At last the party was over.

"Thank you for having Sam build your house. Thank you for having such a nice party!" everyone said. "We've never had so much fun."

The Old Woman waved good-bye from the Attic. "I've never had so much fun either, but I'm tired. I'll put things in order after I have a cup of Tea." Then she sighed. "But I'm too tired to walk to the Tennis court, or to the Quiet room, or even to put my Glasses in the Garage. All I want to do is rock in my Rocking chair, but that's in the *R* room."

Suddenly she remembered. "I never did move the Rocking chair back to the Rumpus room! Sam is so stubborn! Where did he put it? Did he take it back to my old house?" She went down the Attic steps, crossed the grass to her old wee bit of a house, and opened the door.

"Sam!" she cried. "What a perfectly orderly house this is!"

"I thought it was just what you wanted," Sam said. Then he gave her a kiss and whistled his way home.

And Sam was right. It was what she wanted all along. A perfectly orderly house. And perfectly orderly it stayed, from then until forever.